You Think You Want To Be A Florist
Part one

All The books together, Volume 1

Philip Stanworth

Published by Philip Stanworth, 2023.

While every precaution has been taken in the preparation of this book, the publisher assumes no responsibility for errors or omissions, or for damages resulting from the use of the information contained herein.

YOU THINK YOU WANT TO BE A FLORIST PART ONE

First edition. March 25, 2023.

Copyright © 2023 Philip Stanworth.

ISBN: 979-8215769140

Written by Philip Stanworth.

Also by Philip Stanworth

All The books together
A Small Snapshot Of Birds
You Think You Want To Be A Florist Part one
You Think You Want To Be A Florist Part 2
The Good Shepherd & Other Stories
Surprise Days Out With The Kids
The Mansion Through Time
Three Small Stories for 3-4 year olds
Alphabet & Numbers

Standalone
You Think You Want To Be A Florist

Watch for more at https://designs-by-nature.teemill.com/.

<u>You Think You Want To Be A Florist?</u>
Written by- Philip Stanworth
Illustrated by Mrs N Stanworth

<u>You Think You Want To Be A Florist?</u>
Second edition

<u>Check out all our other books</u> https://heartloveart.wixsite.com/website/philip-stanworth-author-all-books

The website is on this QR code
All my socials, all about Philip Stanworth and all my eBook and print book and all the stores you can buy them are all linked to my website above.

There are even toys, children's clothes, bags and more on my website check it out.

<u>Books Written by</u>
<u>Philip Stanworth books &</u>
<u>N Stanworth's books</u>
You Think You Want To Be A Florist Part One
You Think You Want To Be A Florist Part Two
<u>Children's books</u>
Alphabet & Numbers
A Small Snapshot of Birds
The Good Shepherd & Other Stories
The Mansion Through Time Part one
Surprise Days Out With The Kids

<u>You think you want to be a florist?</u>

Floristry/ Florists isn't just for Women because in my experience there are as much Men than women in Floristry

in Europe it is properly more men than women also demonstrators are men as well. If you are good at art you would properly be good at it.

This book explains all about my personal experiences of being in the floristry industry, from

how to I would make the floristry designs for weddings to funerals giving a diagram to construct floristry designs.

Not necessarily how the floristry hand book would tell you.

I have written about personal moments in the floristry industry that are amusing to awkward.

Your Personal use only not to be used as a teaching aid.

This Book is from my own experience in the floristry trade, as a young florist.

These are actual events that have occurred while I have been in the industry.

This is my personal opinion how I have made floristry designs but not necessarily the way they tell you to make them at college.

The information about floral foam is from the internet from scientific journals and veering florists, links are provided.

Content

Chapter One

Being a florist

When you start in a florist shop for the first time, you are completely in their hands, so you trust them. You have been to college, learning the ropes, but you need real-life experience, which is what life is all about.

When you get out there, sometimes people take advantage of you, and sometimes people don't. Some people take you under their wing, which is what you need to help you learn and grow. I have put together some incidents from setting weddings up to various things that could happen to you as a florist

You have to make mistakes, that's how you learn.

As a florist, you have to get up early at peak times. There was one occasion when I came into work I couldn't concentrate, because it was 5.00 am and I had finished at 10.00 am the previous night, so I was walking around like a zombie. Thank God I didn't need to calculate anything, because I wouldn't have got it right. Sometimes as a florist, you could be working 13 hours per day at peak times. I have done 80 hours that week, which was exhausting. I asked to go home one Mothers day, after doing 80hours but the boss said "No you need to carry on" there was no getting out of it. If you think that is floristry is just selling flowers, you need to think again. It involves making heavy handtied's and other heavy things, like picking up buckets with lots of water in them.

<u>Being a florist</u>

The first thing I can tell you about being a florist it isn't as easy as people think, the number of times people have said to me I would love to be a florist I would be a millionaire.

Because people only see what they want to see serving in the flower shop and making handtieds up.

Be a florist isn't that easy you have got to keep up with making handtied's. This involves arranging with your hands all day if you have a lot of orders your hands hurt and if you get expensive handties like £50 that is a lot of flowers to hold.

Next, you have to stand up all day your legs and your hands do get used to this but it takes awhile.

When you are buying off wholesalers or Dutchmen you have to think about how much you are going to sell them for so always look for a good price. Cheap flowers don't always mean good quality flowers.

When the flowers come you need to condition them, this means is you have to take the leaves off stem up to where the water line is going to be also if you are conditioning Roses take the thorns off.

Cut the flowers at an angle because if the stem is cut straight it wouldn't drink the water.

I have heard people saying I have never seen a male florist if you look around England there is quite a lot. When you look in Europe there are more men in the industry than women.

Taking an order as a florist you have to listen to the customer but you have to think about the flowers in the shop if they order it weeks in advice will you be able to order the flowers the customer wants. But if the flowers are out of season you may not be able to order them or they might cost more money.

The next thing is when you are taking an order is your writing is readable and the spelling is right also make sure date and the time is right. You may need to order funeral bases in from
A wholesaler one or two weeks in advance.

Making Christmas Wreaths

I was given all the mossing and materials for making Christmas wreaths. I probably made 160 wreaths a year, They are made up of Spruce, Pine, Holly green with berries and also variegated Holly. I would sometimes put other things running though the wreaths these would all be bound onto the moss wreath. These would usually sell for £25.00 other people would decorate them and get the credit it's the same old story. The doors were always open to showing we were open, in the winter we would have to get out our hats and body warmers working in the cold isn't very nice.

One day I was in the florist on my own and three Gypsies came in and wanted to talk to the boss. So I told them she wasn't in, they said this shop is cursed know. Wow!! Some people can be so in your face.

The conditioning especially is difficult at peak times because you have to get through a lot of it. Most of the flowers come from Holland some come from England not a lot of flowers for the trade come from England it is a shame.

<u>Peak times</u>

Christmas starts quite early because it is spread out into a few months. After Christmas, you have a little break from the madness and jump into Valentine's day you have to prepare a week in advice for this.

The amount of Red Roses you use is staggering especially if you are a member of Interflora. You have about 4 weeks then it is Mothers day – this is the busiest time of the year, Mother day changes every year in England so when you have just got over the madness of Valentines there is not a lot of time until it is Mothers day.

Lastly, you have Christmas again but in-between all of this you have weddings and funerals these can be busy if you have a lot to do.

Every peak time is tiring because you have to stay more hour and more days at work.

I have been in one florist at a busy time making 100 hand-tied bouquets in one day.

Sometimes Easter is busy some places are busy for Jewish New Year.

<u>How long it takes to become a good florist</u>

If you want to become a florist it takes usually 3 years at college and maybe another few years in the industry,

It's all about trust if the head florist trusts you can do the designs you will improve by making things up.

<u>How to set a florist shop out</u>

Lots of different florists are set out in different ways when you are setting a florist. Set out the flowers and colours that go together. Next for Handtied's and gift wrap's flowers that you have made up. Keep them nearest the door so people can look at them, don't feel obliged to ask, keep the prices clear and affordable. Customers will ask if they want anything

more expensive.

Once I went for an interview at a florist. The shop was the size of a box room when I worked there the boss didn't want to clean the floor until the end of the day. Because there was no bin, so I didn't want to stay there the boss said he wanted me to do the flower arrangements exactly like his, so I left.

I have been in lots of florists, in this particular florist at peak times there would be four people doing the conditioning normal days there would be one person doing it.

Sometimes we would have an order from a venue, for Valentine's Day for them to give 150 red Roses to their staff. I had to cut 150 pieces of cellophane on a dry counter. The cellophane had to be long enough to cover the whole stem; the same amount of plastic test tubes had to go on the Roses on the end of the stem. I had to put a bow on all of them, the bows had to be the same size. I put the cellophane on the Rose I had to make sure the Rose could breathe.

My manageress was serving a chap and he came into the back and said to me you are the first male floral display I have ever seen my manager said to him he isn't a floral display he is a florist.

The secret of floristry photography is when you are taking the pictures for the website; you need the arrangement to be just right. That means flowers need to be just at the right stage. If someone has made an arrangement and you see a gap fill the gap in, so the picture looks just right. You have to take the photo at the right angle to get everything in the picture.

I often talked to customers, the lady in question needed some help and she trusted me. One day she came into the florist and asked if I would like to help her she lived next door to the shop. I followed her, I had to pick up a man in a wheelchair over the lip of the door into a porch then lift him over another lip into the main house it was quite a challenge. I came into work the next day, the lady from next door, gave me a gift of white wine. So I thanked her but isn't necessary.

You hear lots of things, which are not necessarily what people want repeating. These stories are from drivers who changed their careers. A driver at the shop was a prison officer before he worked at the florist he told me this story a man had been locked up for killing his wife after killing her he chopped her up and added her to the pies that he sold in his small café.

Then there was another driver who used to be a police traffic officer, he was on patrol on a road accident and he found a full hand on the ground.

How to keep flowers for long periods. If you have lots of flowers or even if you have not of a lot of flowers at home, you always need to remember to have a clean container and add flower food. Do this every other day and recut your flowers at an angle. Keep your flowers in a cool place never put them near a radiator or a window.

<u>Funerals</u>

The way florists should think of funerals is you can do the best for the person who has ordered the flowers.

It's the last thing the customer can do for their loved one so the florist should do the best they can for them. Taking note of special flowers but not getting emotionally involved.

In my experience you don't get double pay for doing more hours then you are supposed to do.

I have worked with people who have had their own shop but it didn't work out for them. Then they come to work for someone else. I was showing a lady how to make a hand-tied who had been a florist for 20 years in her own shop.

Her hand-tied was wrong she kept saying to me "I don't know why I can't do it, I have done it before, It's so sad." She started to tell us how she made everything in her shop. Also, she would criticize our work, when she couldn't make as good as me.

I have also met florists who are nice and just get on with their work. They are nice to the customers and help them out, not because of the money, but because they want to help that person over a funeral or weddings. They try to help them get what they want and listen to the customer. I have known a few people like this, but not many. There should be more florists like this.

Valentine's Day

Two of us made so many handtieds in a few hours, but we had to stay late most days to keep up with demand, starting early and finishing about nine or ten o'clock at night. What you hear from most florists is there is no other way to make money than standing up all day in the cold and getting wet hands. But, other than that, we all love it, cracks and all. I mean the cracks on your hands from being in the cold and wet.

It's a florist joke.

Valentine's Day

There was one chap who came every year and ordered a single red Roses for a woman for the whole year for us to deliver each week of that year.

Every time they were delivered to a woman's house, she asked who are they from, we couldn't tell her because of data protection every week she sent it back with the driver, so this was awkward for us.

Valentines 2019

A driver was driving along normally when the side door fell off, so he tied it on with plastic ribbon until he could get it fixed. Another driver was delivering flowers, she broke down and had to wait around for the

AA to fix the van. Well, you would think that would be all, but it wasn't! I finished my handtieds on the side of the drive because I was working outside. The driver didn't see my hand-tied and he drove over the stems of two of my handtieds. It gets better ! he had parked on top of the stems, I told him to reversed off them! When I got them from under the van I had to change some stems, but not all of them, "What a relief". When I was pricing up the handtieds, the same driver nearly ran me over! So when you are buying your flowers next Valentine's Day, think about what the florists go through.

Every florist shop has a different approach to floristry e.g. there own style and techniques of making. You need to be a caring, sympathetic and artistic person to be a florist.

Mothers Day

When I think of Mothers day, I think it is the busiest time on the florist's calendar. There are so many verities of designs you can sell from normal handtieds, baskets spring flowers they are all nice it is better having a nice selection of flower designs. I would prefer Mothers day than any other peak time because there is so much choice to make than any other peak times.

Christmas

Christmas in a florist usually starts in October getting everything ready someone used to tell me to be prepared or be prepared to fail. You have to moss the Christmas wreaths ready for you to put the different foliages on them. Then you have to have all the Pinecones, dried Oranges, dried limes wired to put into things. When it gets cold it makes it harder to make things because you are trying to keep warm.

As a florist, you have to make so much that sometimes makes your arms sore, because you are making large and small handtieds. For example, I made a tropical hand-tied it included 12 Ginger flowers, 12 Aspidistra's, 3 large Heliconias and small Heliconias, I had to make two of these handtieds, which made my hands very sore. So, if you are spending a lot of money on one hand-tied maybe ask for an arrangement or a vase arrangement because large handtieds are very hard on the florist's hands.

The term conditioning is used by florists, it means to take the foliage off the bottom of the flower and cut the flower or foliage at the bottom at an angle so they take in more water if they are cutting it straight the water doesn't go up the stem as good as it is sitting at the bottom of the vase etc.

The best thing about floristry is when you have made some sympathy flowers and the people come back and thank you. For something you have made and tell you it has made a difference, well I think that is it is so important to put your life and soul into this for these moments.

You have to love floristry to be in it because it is a love-hate sort of job.

When you think of peak times such as Valentine's Day, Mothers Day, Jewish New Year and especially Christmas

Chapter Two
How to make funeral Designs
& Amusing Moments
<u>Funeral Designs</u>

The most important thing about doing funeral work is this is the last thing you can do for a person. Taking a funeral order, most important information is the date and the time if it is an early funeral i.e. 8.00 am send it out the night before to the funeral directors.

When you are taking a funeral order listen carefully because you don't want to get anything wrong especially for a funeral.

When you have got all the important information done with, let them look at pictures, leave them to look on their own when they are ready they will come over to you.

Sometimes they will need you to guide them, help out with what flowers are available at the time of year also if the colours are available. If they are after a double-ended show them with a tape measure because some people can't visualise how big something can be. If you have something made up in the shop like the design show it to them.

When you have taken the order off them say take care I never say with the deepest sympathy or anything like that you don't want to set them off. Because they will be very sensitive, just be kind and respectful. If they start telling you about the person who has died be patient and listen.

I look at it if you get too upset about the person, you won't do your best work for the customer.

A customer came into the shop with a Labrador with a yellow banner on it so I presumed he was blind. He asked me what colour Roses you have so I told him, to my surprise! he pointed out to the yellow Roses. This has taught me never to presume anything.

A customer came into the shop with his son, he asked me could this hand-tied be reduced by £5.00, please my son has only got £25.00. I said to the customer I'm sorry this isn't my shop so I can't do that but I can make a similar bouquet but with fewer flowers in it. He changed his mind saying "O blow it I will take them", " I will pay the extra £5.00".

There was one florist whom I knew, who won competitions nearly all the time she was a wedding contractor. Yet her shop arrangements, including the handtieds, were awful! How can you do all that, but not be able to do basic floristry?

An oriental lady brought a hand-tied off the front. My colleague asked me to come and help her, the customer couldn't speak English! she was pointing to a picture in the shop. We thought that the lady wanted the hand-tied to be similar but we didn't have the flowers. The lady started to pull the tissue paper out of the hand-tied bag which was lime green, the lady was pointing at red tissue paper so I changed it. She bought the hand-tied, I bowed to her being respectful when the lady had left the shop, my colleague burst out laughing at me.

<u>Funeral Designs</u>
Double-ended
When you are greening the double-ended up you have to think of it is
the skeleton of the design
To start I am going to show you the shape you are going to be aiming for
An elongated diamond shape
I usually start with the Palm leaves next I put Leather Leaf in to make
this shape
You need to get the length first with your Palms or any long thin foliage
then you add some foliage for the width in the middle folded
Aspidistra's, Salal and Eucalyptus going through the design
Don't put too much foliage in so you can't get the flowers in, because
you can put more foliage in when you have flowers in.
<u>Double-ended</u>
2ft-3ft design
Soak 1 ½ blocks of floral foam until they are heavy that is when you
know they are soaked. When they are soaked, place the full block on the
bottom and the ½ a block at the top put them on a single floral foam
tray tape it on with pot tape so it is nice and secure
<u>For a 4ft design</u>
2 ½ blocks of floral foam when they are soaked put them on a double
tray and put the half a block in the centre of the 2 blocks and tape it on
securely
5ft - 6ft design
4 block of floral foam cut one lengthways put the 3 on a three-block tray
and put the 2 half's in the centre
The reason you put the blocks on top of other floral foam is to give it
more height when you are making the design.
<u>Double-ended</u>
For an all Rose double-ended size 4ft-5ft-6ft
Sundries you will need - florist Scissors, floral foam, pot tape and a floral
foam tray

<u>For a 4ft double ended –</u>
60 large-headed Roses, Palms 14, Leather leaf 1 bunch; Eucalyptus roughly 3 bunches 6 Aspidistras and Salal to fill in.
Then for a 5ft or 6ft-
70 large-headed Roses, Palm leaves 18 the same as above with foliage
On the first pages of double ended's I have made a list of how much floral foam to use for each size.

<u>Double-ended</u>

<u>All Lilly</u>

Before you make this design you need to keep the lilies somewhere warm for them to
open, take the pollen out of the flower head. This needs to be done because of the pollen can stain the flowers and it is a nightmare to get it off the flower head.
You might need more if you are using Asiatic lilies because they are smaller heads and you can't split the stem to make the shape.
You will need to have properly about 15 with Oriental lily's for a 4ft for a 5-6 foot you need properly about 20 lilies.
Firstly make the shape with foliage next start adding the longest lilies first
Cut off one or 2 of the open Lily heads off the stem, use them for the centre of the design.
You need to put the buds around the edge cut the lily in ½ so you have 2 heads on each
Carry on with that method until you have finished. Put buds in the centre of the design in-between the open heads then put Eucalyptus in-between to fill in the gaps so you can't see the floral foam.

<u>Double-ended</u>
<u>Bespoke design</u>
You go with flowers and colours that match then if your client has seen a style they like to go off that style then work around that.
So for a suggestion Spring theme
You would use Roses, Solidago or goldenrod then add in tulips, Hyacinth's, and other spring flowers bulb flowers. Gerberas
When putting these sorts of flowers in floral foam they need wiring or putting wire up the stem.
Choosing your flowers but remember to place the largest flowers in the centre of the design.
For a stylish design use only 2 -3 flowers all Rose or Roses and Lilies
But all depends on the colour lots of different flowers go together if you are going with a vibrant design use different colours, but even if you are going to make a monochromatic design with only one colour this looks equally as nice. But you are going for an open and full design equally spaced out because the flowers need to have gaps in-between to make an overall nice design.
<u>Styles</u>
<u>If you are going modern</u>
Use tropical flowers Anthriums, Birds of paradise and other tropical flowers, tropical foliage and sticks to enhance your design.
<u>Single-ended spray</u>
There are 2 types of single ended's
One with stems coming out the back of the design to make it look like a sheaf.
Second there are ones looking like a teardrop shape
When I had finished college, I was working my colleague put her fleece on my bench. I thought it was my fleece, so I picked it up and went into the car. I got a phone call from my colleague saying "Have you got the keys to my car and house?" I replied "yes" we had to drive back

15miles. The look on my colleague's face was priceless, so I smiled and said: "I will see you tomorrow".

I was delivering some flowers to the house of a well-known customer across the road. I went to the house, knocked on the door, used the bell then waited 5 minutes. Looked through the window and saw the man, I waved at him he looked at me, then went to get some breakfast. I knocked again on the door. After about 10 minutes, I was about to go back to the shop, the woman of the house came to answer the door took the flowers of me and didn't say anything.

I was making an order, it was a vase arrangement. The card and the envelope were written, but I needed some more flowers, I put the card onto the fork and placed it into the vase of broken flowers on my desk so it wouldn't get misplaced. I nipped into the shop for the fresh flowers for the arrangement, to my horror I find that the driver had taken the vase of broken flowers to be delivered. The driver seemed to have no idea the flowers he took were half dead. Luckily I rang the driver before he delivered them to tell him to come back for the fresh vase arrangement.

A colleague and I were making Christmas wreaths. We had about 150 wreaths to do and we started to chat. I said "It's great doing this isn't it" he replied, "This isn't floristry. It's more like slave labour. There is no creativity and it's very tedious."

Bin Story

As I was working a lady came to look around to where the bins where and asked me how much is this flower, it was out of the bin I replied they aren't for sale there are some fresher flowers in the shop.

The shop I was working at the time had a large dog sometimes; I would have to hold him. On occasions, I would get dragged down the shop "I don't think this was in my job decryption".

There was a customer who came into have three arrangements made up, which he wanted every other week. He brought a picture and said, "You can make them off this picture." However, when you go to a florist, you need to let the florist have some artistic licence not just to copy it off a picture.

<u>Sheaf's</u>
<u>Open Sheaf</u>
Modern

You can use Calla Lilies and Roses with foliage and keep it in a line with both flowers going thought the design. You can do this with a lot of different flowers e.g.

Birds of Paradise in a line but you need to have distinctive foliage such as Aspidistras going through the design for a more modern look.

But when you are going traditional you need to go with mixed flowers such as Rose, Chrysanthemums, open Lilies, Carnations, spray carnations.

So when you start a traditional sheaf you need to have a strong stem of foliage to start with for the backing e.g. Palm leaves with Salal to support the design then when you add the flowers

I usually go with flowers with such as flowers that are still quite tight and not opened

Lilies or Roses so you have a defined point, go down the design adding foliage and other flowers that are more open to bulk the sheaf out.

When you are doing this you need to add foliage you will get a better and more open design if you make the Sheaf on the bench.

You are going for a triangle shape. When you about to finish it off you need to check if the sheaf is wide enough so its looks good value for the money then you put foliage at the bottom to protect the flowers. There are 2 different types of sheaf's ones in cellophane and ones without I prefer the flowers out of cellophane because it shows the flowers off to at their best.

<u>Sheaf's</u>

With any floristry, it needs practice, practice, practice. You will get quicker and that is what shops want you to do a good job but have speed.

When you are taking the order make sure the customer knows the difference between an open sheaf and the sheaf in cellophane, when they come to collect this if they haven't understood the difference they will expect the sheaf in cellophane as they think that is the bag for the flowers to be taken in.

I took an order for an open sheaf and explained what it would be like e.g. without cellophane. The customer came to collect it but she hadn't understood, I had to take the bow off the sheaf and put it into the cellophane with the customer watching me. This seems funny now but when you have the customer watching you it is awkward because the customer expected the flowers to be in cellophane.

I completed the Level 2 Floristry course the day before Mother's Day, as I had done 40hours of college studies, required for working in the industry.

In my first job, they wouldn't let me do much, so I said "I won't be coming back because you hardly allowed me to do anything" the shop owner replied snappily "You won't be able to do this when you are working as a full- time florist". I quickly replied "I would do this if I was getting paid and treated better. Good-bye"

I went into the shop and this lady was looking at the red Roses. The customer said to me which Rose is the lightest?? I replied all of them, I asked her why she replied it is going to be part of my Halloween costume I am going to glue the Rose to the middle of my forehead?.

One man came into the florist. He liked the arrangement in the shop and he started to barter with me. So I said to him, "Sorry Sir". You can't barter. We aren't in an auction room. I'm sorry, but you will have to pay the full price".

One occasion a customer came back with some flowers, complaining that they had died after a week. As a goodwill gesture, we replaced them. To our amazement he came back after another 7 days and complaining they had died, we should have sold him artificial ones.

One customer came in and said "The way I like the arrangements to be delivered is, if it is windy or raining, you need to reverse into the driveway, when you take them out of the van, take them out very slowly.

My boss made a long Rose arrangement one night. It was about 7ft when she came in the next morning all the Roses were dead she hadn't put enough water in the floral foam.

A colleague was serving a customer; she forgot to take the price ticket out of the flowers. So when the customer was leaving I said to my colleague is the price still in that hand-tied so she ran down the shop to take the price ticket out. She came back smiling and looked relieved.

I had a customer for who had three orchid planters and came in every couple of mouths. She had been getting them for years; she had been advised on how to care for them. However, every time the planters came back they were dead over watered. It's funny and ironic at the same time.

<u>Posy arrangement</u>
<u>A posy arrangement shape is a circle</u>
<u>You will need</u>
½ a block of floral foam, a posy dish, pot tape, leather leaf
Tape the soaked floral foam into the dish so it is tight this is when you have soaked it.
You go around the edge of the pad with foliage most often or not it is leather leaf but you can use anything from the garden to make a circle shape. Next focus on the middle you're your design with putting your focal flowers in then have the less expensive flowers your filler flowers around the outside to make your shape.
Focal flowers, Rose's, Carnation's, Gemini's, to get your shape Carnation Spray
And finally filler flowers, Freesias, Chrysanthemum's spray and Gypsophilia.
There are ready-made posy pads they range from 10inch to 14 inches depending on how big you want a design. This is for more expensive designs.

It was the end of the day; I was going to get some glass from the shed I discovered the padlock was cut and a lot of broken glass all over the floor. So the police came, the funny thing was there was a hat that looked like our colleagues in the shed, we were all asked as a group by the police. About 15 minutes later the policeman let us go.

Cows in the Road

A colleague and I went to another florist in Ramsbottom, to collect some sundries for the stock room. On our way back to the shop, a herd of cows came out of nowhere and blocked the road. We waited for about 10 minutes, for the cows to move.

Christmas tree Catastrophe

My Colleague and I went to a venue to put up a Christmas tree. When we saw it, we were shocked because the size was wrong. We had received a 6ft tree when we were supposed to have a 14ft tree. What happened was we put the tree onto a small round table which we covered with a red cloth, to match the decorations. We didn't panic; we just got on with it.

You often get customers saying to you "This must be a fantastic job, playing with flowers all the time" You would like to say, "Yes, if you only knew what we have done to get the flowers ready, such as standing in the cold, working with the door open all hours, putting your hands in cold water in all weathers standing in the cold and wet, Yes it is great?? "It has some good points, though- the flowers? That is the best point".

One Valentine's Day a man came into the shop and stole a bunch of small Roses. My Colleague saw him do this, so she ran after him and said to him, "Come back!", but he ran off, so she chased him out of the shop and down the street, until she caught him. The man looked very rough but thankfully, she got the flowers off him and came back unharmed.

<u>Posy arrangement</u>
<u>Grouped</u>
<u>You will need</u>
Posy pad 12inch
<u>Foliages</u>
Mixed foliages e.g. Pittosporum, Hypericum, Eucalyptus, Leather leaf
<u>Flowers</u>
Roses x 2, Dill x2 or Bluplurum, Spider Chrysanthemum x2,
Onithegalum x2 and Carnations x 10
<u>Construction</u>
Soak your posy pad, place your mixed foliages into groups to create a circle domed shape. Putting any foliage that is available because it is classed as a natural design.

Next place your flowers into your design place your 2 Roses off centre, place your groups of Carnations 2 in a group for your central flower. Put the 2 groups of 3 carnations around the outside of the design in both sides of the design place your last group of Carnations in a group of 2.

These sections try and make it into a triangle shape then put the Onithegalum or Chincherinchee place you group of 2 in-between the Carnations. Place Dill though the design then lastly use the Chrysanthemum in groups to finish your design.

<u>Letters</u>
Some customers want the name of the person spelling out with flowers e.g. Mum, Nan, excreta. Each letter is made out of floral foam. There are letters you can buy already made up

Such as Mum, Dad such as fixed titles like this but when you come to people's names you have to buy the letters individually and buy plastic poles to attach the letters onto them.

Before you fix them onto the pole you need to soak the letters, when attaching the letters spread them out enough so they are readable when you have made the design, when you have placed the letters in the right position tape them onto the pole.

There are 2 designs you can do with letters there are loose letter and massed I have explained more about them below.

<u>Loose Letters</u>

When you are doing a loose design you need to go with a colour theme and have lots of small dainty flowers. To fill in but you need focal flowers like Gemini's or Roses.

When you have soaked your letters first define the shape of the letter with Leather Leaf or Arachnoides Adiantiformis brake into small manageable pieces you can outline the letter. Fill the whole letter with the foliage then add the focal flowers then you fill in with smaller flower this can become a tedious job to do but at the end, it looks well worth the time you spent on it.

<u>Massed Letters</u>

When you have soaked your letters have some smaller blocks to put onto the letter at the bottom if you are doing MUM usually I would put the spray left bottom of the M then on the other M I would put it on the right so the design is balanced. So you need to tape them on so they secure but so you can get the flowers on later so use thin pot tape. With massed letters, florists usually go with the traditional technique to define the shape

Which is pleating some plastic ribbon so they are groups of squares it takes a long time to get good at this technique and it is difficult to explain on paper so the way I am going to explain is use foliage such as Leather leaf to define the shape of the letter.

Next thing is to add the flowers with no space in-between this is called massing You will need approximately 15 to 20 bunches of Spray Chrysanthemum for MUM depending how big the Chrysanthemum White Double heads are so getting more in then you need if the heads are small.

Firstly when you are massing it takes a lot of Chrysanthemum heads cut all the heads onto your desk, put the medium size heads around the letter then work inwards but you need to keep the shape of the letter and flower heads so it looks 3D that is your aim. When you have done this you need to do the sprays so you have got the 2 small pieces of floral foam on either side of the design I like to put a smaller spray in the U at the bottom in the middle just 1 flower out of the sprays. Usually, you put 3 roses and filler flowers; add bear grass to link the 3 sprays together.

<u>Funeral Designs</u>
<u>Gypsophilia Heart</u>
You will need a 10" Heart

<u>Construction</u>
1 pack of Gyp roughly about 20 stems depending on how big the Gyp is Soak the Heart under a tap or have a bowl and have water in it and leave it to soak in this.
Firstly cut a few stems up then group little bits of Gypsophilia together then get 2 fingers worth of flowers group together then put them into the heart around the edge then carry onto the middle.

<u>Single Heart Massed</u>
<u>You will need</u>
Heart foundation 12inches
Pot tape
Spray Chrysanthemum- White double roughly 10 bunches depending on flower size
Oasis
Roses, Singapore Orchids
Leather leaf

<u>Construction</u>
Soak your Heart foundation attach a block of floral foam roughly 4inchs long and 3 inches wide attach it to the side of the heart and tape it securely on.
Cut the head of the Chrysanthemum stem
Go around the side of the heart with the Spray Chrysanthemum keeping the flowers tight to the sides of the design.
Next, go into the centre of the design making it domed

define the heart shape keeping the Chrysanthemum tight to design, if there is any small gaps fill them in with the smaller heads of the Chrysanthemum.

Lastly use the Leather leaf to green your small piece of oasis to create the focal point of your design. Add your flowers such as Roses for your focal point and Singapore Orchids to go through the spray.

<u>Single Heart Loose</u>
<u>You will need</u>
Heart foundation
Foliage e.g. Leather Leaf, Bear Grass
Carnations - 16
Gemini's- 10
Roses -7
<u>Construction</u>

Soak the heart foundation next green around the heart to create a good base to add the flowers into your design.

Starting with Carnations the around the edge of the design with foliage in-between the Carnations.

Next use the Germini's and put them around the design following the Carnations. Fill the centre of the heart with Roses add the Bear Grass to define the Heart shape over the top of the flowers wiring the grass into the foam to keep it secure.

<u>Loose Heart</u>
<u>You will need</u>
Foliage Pittosporum //Carnations -12
Roses – 6// Spray Carnations - 5
Spray Chrysanthemums- 3 stems
<u>Construction</u>

Soak the heart foundation under a tap, green you heart keeping to the shape of the design. Next place the Carnations around the edge of the design to create the shape of the design then use them as the focal flower of the design. Place the Roses in-between the Carnations in the centre of the design.

Lastly use the Carnation Spray and the Spray Chrysanthemums to fill in your design.

<u>Double Heart grouped design</u>

<u>You will need</u>

A double heart foundation, German pins

Moss, Mixed foliages , Dill x5 stems

A mix of different coloured Roses 15 in total, Cymbidium Orchid – a mini stem x1 stems

Lisanthus x2 stems ,Carnation's x5, Statice x2 large stems and Eryngium x2 stems

<u>Construction</u>

Soak you Heart foundation /Pin moss all around the edge of the design put the moss in different areas around your design in clusters. Use different foliages in groups though out the design but don't green it all over because the flowers need to go into the design.

When adding your flowers into your design keep. them groups of 2 or 3 flower heads.

Add the Carnations and the Dill though the design in-between the other flowers.

<u>Wreath ring</u>

<u>Massed</u>

<u>You will need</u>

Wreath ring , Pot tape , Floral foam

Leather Leaf, Spray Chrysanthemum White Double , Roses and Spray Carnations

<u>Construction</u>

Soak the wreath, attach your small piece of floral foam to make a small arrangement roughly 3inchs long 2inches wide use the pot tape to make sure you secure it on to the wreath ring.

Define the shape by using foliage such as Leather leaf around the edge of the wreath.

Go around the wreath ring with the spray Chrysanthemums keeping the flower heads close together. Continue by adding the flower heads making a domed shape place them inside the wreath ring finishing this part of the design.

Next part of the design is to green up the small piece of floral foam to make this the focal point of the design.

Add the focal flower such as Roses making a line then to fill with the Spray Carnations or any filler flowers.

<u>Loose Wreath ring</u>

<u>You will need</u>

A wreath ring, mixed foliages , 2 focal flower e.g. Carnations and Roses Filler flowers- Spray Carnations anything you can break up and use in your design

<u>Construction</u>

Soak your wreath ring, green the wreath up to create a domed shape with the foliage. Then place the filler flowers in to define the shape such as the Spray Carnations and the Spray Chrysanthemums.

Add the focal flowers in place keeping foliage in-between them spreading the flowers out.

You usually use 2 different focal flowers to add interest then fill in with another filler flower go through the design.

<u>Crosses</u>

There are different styles of doing crosses in floral foam so massed cross and loose cross,

Modern Cross and lastly a biodegradable cross just made out of sticks with flowers added

You can get a lot of sizes and styles of crosses there are a few different examples I have explained below

<u>Massed</u>

<u>You will need</u>

Cross Foundation, 1/3 of a block of floral foam, Spray
Chrysanthemum, Leather leaf

<u>Construction</u>

Soak the Cross foundation then soak the 1/3 of a block of floral foam
tape to the centre of the cross.

Define the cross shape with the Leather leaf or other foliage then go
around the cross with the large-headed flowers then continue until you
have finished massing the design then go over the cross and see if it
needs filling in use the smaller headed Chrysanthemum's.

When you start on the 1/3 of a block of floral foam make the focal
point start with the length with some soft Ruckus then fill the rest of
the floral foam in. Next, put the flowers in
I usually use Calla Lilies for this design because they have a good thin
flower
for the length then when you get into the middle of the cross-use
Roses for a nice focal point.

<u>Crosses</u>

<u>Loose</u>

Firstly get some good foliage to fill in the Cross such as Leather leaf,
Pistache, Eucalyptus and fill it in. fill in with the smaller flowers such as
Wax flower, Soldiage use them as foliage and fill it in all over the place
then get the focal flowers in then put some Chrysanthemum spray heads
going all over the design. Keep adding flowers until it looks finished they
always look that they need more so keep adding until you think it looks
right.

<u>Modern Cross -Aspidistra Cross</u>
<u>You will need</u>
A cross foundation, Aspidistra leaves, Orchids, Roses
When you are making this design don't do it a week in advance because some stems aren't going to be in the oasis i.e., not drinking water.
<u>Construction</u>
Soak the cross and 1/3 block of floral foam tape it on to the cross foundation.
Cut the Aspidistra up into strips to go around the side of the Cross use the German pins to keep it in place. Do this around the cross, when you are putting the pins in place them so they are hidden, place the top leaves so they are overlapped. Pin the leaves under the overlapped area's so the Aspidistras stay in place.
As it is a modern design you need to use modern flowers Roses and Orchids if you are using Phalaenopsis orchids and you want to use just the head use the small test tubes on the stems , spread the flowers out and us veering flowers such as Roses then you get a 2 tone look.
<u>Crosses</u>
<u>Stick Cross in floral foam</u>
You will need silver birch sticks quite a lot
String // 2/3rds of floral foam, A single floral foam tray //Soft foliage for the length such as Soft Ruckus & Leather leaf
<u>Construction</u>
Soak the floral foam put it in the middle of the tray and tape it in firstly
Get a group of sticks and tie them together with string and get the length usually, it is 3ft for the length then for the arms it is 2ft but you need a good grouping of sticks for a good effect.
Fill in-between the sticks with foliage not distracting from the shape of the cross.
Fill in the centre of the design with the flowers keeping with the overall shape of the cross.
<u>Crosses</u>

<u>Biodegradable Cross - made out of sticks and string</u>
Bamboo
Contorted Hazel Stick
String
Roses and foliage

Group some bamboo so the main part is roughly about 3ft for the length bind this group together so it is secure, next do a smaller grouping for the arms so they measure roughly about 2ft bind it together. Attach these 2 groups to make a cross shape attach them with string.

Attach some Contorted Hazel to the centre of the cross with string to give more shape to the design.

Make a little bunch of Roses and Anthriums with some soft Ruckus so you have got the length then tie it to the centre of the cross.

<u>Vegetative Arrangement</u>
<u>You will need</u>
1- wreath ring, German pins
Sticks – Contorted Hazel with leaves on them , Flat Moss
If you are doing a spring flower design Ranunculus, Tulips, Anemone,
Heather or Erica
Foliage such as Ivy leaves or any foliage
<u>Construction</u>
Soak your wreath, add your foliages to give the effect that they are
growing so think wild with design keep the flowers in groups.
When you are adding your Moss secure it with the German pins lastly
add your sticks to add interest keep the leaves so you trying to give the
effect of a tree.
The next section is putting your flowers into the design I have gone for
spring flowers for this design but you can use flowers that you any
flowers but I would avoid using Lilies in this design you need nice
straight lines.
<u>Basket Arrangements</u>
<u>You will need</u>
A Basket , floral foam, cellophane, wire or Pot tape foliage leather leaf,
Salal and Eucalyptus
<u>Flowers</u>
Focal flower e.g. Gemini's, Roses, Spray, Carnations ,Spray
Chrysanthemums, Spray Roses.
There are 2 styles of basket arrangement
The first style is the all-round design it is like a posy arrangement but it
is in a basket
Then the next style is a long and low arrangement in a basket usually
using a trug basket.
<u>Construction</u>
The first style- all round design in a basket

Soak about two- thirds of floral foam, when soaked use the cellophane and line your basket, use a wire or pot tape secure the floral foam into the basket if you are using a wire go over the floral foam twice to make sure it is secure then if you are using the pot tape do the same method.

Make an all-round arrangement by putting mixed foliage described above, making a circle shape, use your filler flower around the edge of the design to make the shape. Place your larger flowers around the edge to define the shape of the design, next place the focal flower into the centre, finish by filling with smaller flowers and foliage look over the overall design if it is domed shaped.

<u>The second style- long and low Basket Arrangement</u>

When using the floral foam in this design it depends how long is your design is going to be.

If you are going to make a short design use two thirds and if you are going to make a longer design use a full block.

First, put the cellophane into your basket and place your floral foam over the top and secure it with the wire over the top of it. Make your length with your foliage, next make your shape of the design it will be like a diamond shape like the double-ended spray. Next place longer flowers such as the Roses and the Carnations to create the shape.

Go through the design placing the flowers in the centre of the design creating a long domed shape keeping foliage in-between the flowers so the flowers are spread out.

I was upstairs when a candelabra fell though a gap, looked downstairs quickly. I shouted "Watch out!" what happened next wasn't very nice it landed on my colleague. To save herself she covered her head with her arms. Luckily, it only sprained her arm, as it could have easily knocked her out or worse.

A customer came into the florist, he wanted to buy a gift for his girlfriend she was 18 and he was in his 50's. Well, every fibre in my body was telling me to ring the police and arrest him, but you have to get your professional head on and remind yourself that it isn't any of your business.

It was the end of the day when a man came in he wanted to have 12 red Roses in a hand-tied. I started to make it up when it was nearly finished, he went to the counter to pay, he pulled out a £50 note. My colleague quickly said, "Sorry Sir, we don't take them." He replied, "There are no cash machines nearby" so he left, I had to put the Roses back into stock. He wasn't pleased with us! It was the policy of the shop not to except £50 notes because they might be fakes.

Chapter 3
Gift
Hand-tied
There are 2 ways of doing handtieds
Everyone has their own style so a person could have the same flowers
and still do something different
When you think of Handtieds they are most often used in the floristry
world as a quick sale,
So they are used for everything normal times and especially peak time
that is when you have to do lots of the same one, so you have to do
about maybe about 100 a day at peak time depending on where the
shop is based. So with practise comes speed, if you are not fast you will
be there all night.
You need to have speed but you need consistency with the hand-tied
and the wrapping.
When you are making any hand-tied always think would I want this
think about the price but always think of presentation if you don't like it
why should the customer like it?
When you are taking an order for a hand-tied ask if the person who the
flowers are for is allergic to Lilly's or they have cats because the pollen
can kill the cat.

A man came into the shop asking if he could have a hand-tied in water. His attitude was implying right that second he started to talk to my manageress, she stopped talking to him because he wasn't being very nice. He pointed at me saying you're not a florist are you I replied yes I am, the man replied your friend isn't very nice is she meaning my manageress so I said nothing. He was very blunt saying can you push these two hand tied's together to make one hand-tied. I said to him it isn't as easy as that, it would be quicker if I made it with new flowers. As he wanted to spend £50 so I told him the Dutchmen haven't arrived and there weren't enough flowers in the shop to make a £50 hand-tied. The man started to punch his hand and said I want to have it done know, so I repeated the Dutchmen will be about 1hour and it will take 30miniets to put it together, I went to see if the Dutchmen had arrived unfortunately he hadn't, I went back to the shop. I got back into the shop sneaked past him because he was looking the other way he was the sort of guy who would beat someone up. So I got into the workroom and hid behind the door, I let my Manageress talk to him she told him it would take another 25mins when he was gone she said to me was you hiding I smiled and said yes. My manageress replied saying you wouldn't be any good in a serious incident, you wouldn't protect me I replied: "you are right about that". I went around to see if the Dutchmen had arrived I got some flowers, got back to the shop and my Manageress made the hand-tied. Luckily he didn't come back for about 1hour and I wasn't there at the time. I was thinking about getting the security it was that bad being beaten up it wasn't in my job description.

<u>Front-facing Hand-tied's</u>
<u>Modern</u>
When you are doing a front-facing design you need to have tropical flowers such as Cymbidium Orchids with Roses add big flowers such as lilies there are lots of different flowers you can use but you need to have all the flowers straight so they are facing forward. You just put the stems flush on top on each other
<u>All-round</u>
When you are making an all-round hand-tied you have to put some foliage to start the design then put the focal flower into the foliage then add flowers around that flower but when you are putting them into your hand you need to turn your hand 360 degrease you so keep turning the hand-tied so the stems are spiralled so the stems don't get crushed.
<u>Modern</u>
When you making a modern Handtied you want a good selection of modern and traditional flowers but mix it up so it looks unusual add different foliages folded leaves experiment
<u>Traditional</u>
But when you are making an all traditional hand-tied you need to put bulky flowers such as Gypsophilia, Chrysanthemum's, Roses, and Lilies there are a lot of traditional flowers so you need to go with a colour scheme and flowers that match.
It takes a long time to get good at making hand-tied.

<u>How to make a Gift Handtied</u>
<u>You will need</u>
Salal foliage
Eucalyptus
Mixed flowers keep the flowers same flower to groups of two's or threes, one focal flower
Cellophane or brown craft paper, Cello- tape and String

<u>Construction</u>

Get your focal flower in your hand add some Salal keep your hand low down then put your next flower in at an angle and turn the flowers 360 degrease so the stems aren't pressing together. Add some flowers and add different foliages in-between you want to make the design to look as big as you can. Put some foliage around the edge of the design to keep the stems safe so when you tie the flowers with string tight enough so you aren't breaking the stems.

Cut the stems on an angle keep them long enough for the flowers to go into a vase.

Wrapping your hand-tied

You will need some Cellophane or Brown Craft paper

You need pieces of paper approximately 2 foot and you fold sideways so you have 4 corners or points do the same with the other piece. Use the wrapping you have folded, place it around the hand-tied then use cello tape to secure them in place not too tight so the flowers can breathe then put the string around the binding point.

If you are putting it into a bubble wrap get a square piece of cellophane and place it onto the bottom of the stems of your hand-tied use your other hand to gather it up, make sure all the cellophane is in your hand so when you tie it off and pour water into the cellophane so the water doesn't go everywhere, then place it into a gift bag.

This was my second Mothers Day, I had to get into town, it was Saturday I ordered my taxi, but he came late so I missed the bus to the florist so he said to me "I am going that way, so you can stay in the taxi". He took me 15miles and dropped me outside the florist. I thanked him, he said to me "Don't forget me; I will come in to collect something in the future. Luckily he never did.

<u>Mother's day 2019</u>

The Dutchman was stopped by the police on suspicion of having drugs in the flower wagon, on the way of bringing our flowers. The boss rang him to see where he was and he found out that he was in police custody. Hours later he was released after having his wagon searched but they only found his pack of duty-free cigarettes, but it threw us back quite a bit.

I was in the shop one day and I went down to the front when I saw a lady coming into the shop, but she tripped on the step. She went straight onto her face and banged her head. You could hear it bang on the tiled floor, I went to assist her, two colleagues came and helped her to her feet. I went to get something to clean her cut, I was about to ask her, "Do we need to phone someone to take you home?" My boss said "I will take you to the hospital in your car" so my boss took her to her friend's house in the customer's car and her friend took her to the hospital, the lady's friend phoned later to tell us that she was ok.

<u>Corporate designs</u>

When you are planning for a corporate design you have to think what temperature is where it is going how long they want the design and what do they want such as an arrangement or planted arrangement. Sometimes the client wants plants not flowers so you could do Orchid planter in a nice container. Most often than not it is a flower arrangement they want so you have a weekly design, So you will need a few different vases so they aren't having the same one all the time, What colours do they like? Always give them long-lasting flowers such as tropical flowers because you don't want them to be disappointed if they are going to come back to you every week.

If you are going with an arrangement

<u>You will need</u>
Vases with no transparency
floral foam– Pot tape
Usually tropical flowers
Such as Anthodium's, Birds of Paradise and other tropical flowers
Tropical foliages

<u>Construction of the design</u>
Soak the floral foam place it into the vase secure it in the vase by taping it in with the pot tape. Don't have too much floral foam protruding out of your container showing because you will need to cover it with some flowers.
Green the floral foam with tropical foliage fold the leaves then add the tropical flowers,
keep the design a front-facing design and limited how many flowers you put in the design.
Always put your business card on the design.
This design is also a good advertisement for you so you want the flowers to last for the week.
A sign nearly fell on someone! Imagine a 12ft mettle sign, attached to a mettle pole, One day the wind was blowing so strongly that the sign snapped and crashed to the floor. It was a good thing that it didn't fall onto someone's head.

I was off for a week when I came back my colleagues told me people from "Take Me Out" TV show had been in, asking if there was anyone single in the shop to come onto their show. When I got my chance to talk, I sadly declined because I don't like being in front lots of people on stage never mind being on TV in front of millions of people.

There was a job interview and the chap seemed to be good with his floristry. But he said "I put in extra flowers if it is needed and don't charge for it, I don't take phone calls or serve because it distracts from my creative flow?? Well, he didn't get the job.

At Christmas, there was a woman who would come into the shop with her 2 dogs and wandered around the shop for about 15 minutes before closing time, but we wouldn't close and turn someone away. She was looking for the reduced items and only took 2 things and would take forever looking. Then she would start talking to me about nonsense then she would go after wasting my time?

<u>Christmas</u>

When you are preparing for Christmas you have to do door wreaths at the mid-October if you sell quite a lot I have been in a place where they sold about 270 every year. So you need to moss up all the wreaths. Keep them moist by watering them, the foliage makes the wreath there are two ways the collage way which is slow and the shop way is faster.

<u>How to make a Mossed Wreath</u>
You will need
A bag of Moss Sphagnum ,10" or 12" wire wreath ring, Bobbin wire thick mossing wire
Foliage such as Spruce, Holly, Pine and Conifer
<u>Construction</u>
Start with your wreath and attaching the bobbin wire onto the mettle wreath ring.

Next, grab a handful of moss and place it onto the wreath ring, wrap the bobbin wire around it keep secure then place the next piece overlapping the first lot of moss next wrap the bobbin wire around the moss until you have completed this part of the wreath. Make sure the bobbin wire is pulled tight. To create your wreath you will need to cut your foliages to a good size for use so they can fit in your hand then get the mixed foliage into a group then place them onto an angle, bind the group onto the wreath to be facing into the middle and spared the foliage out then get another grouping of foliage and face it to the outside of the wreath and spread it out. Keep alternating from the outside of the wreath and the inside of the wreath until you have finished the design pull the bobbin wire tight secure it to the wreath ring. Lastly, look at the overall shape it should be a circle design if not wire some foliage and place it into the area that stands out that is wrong until it is a circle shape.

Then when decorating it
For natural <u>Normal</u>
Dried Oranges full and slices Burbles
Pine cones Ribbon bows

It was nearly Christmas, I told my boss my sister had a Holly tree, that needed cutting down. My boss sent the drivers to cut the Holly tree she thought it was a small tree, the drivers cut a lot of branches off but didn't cut it down it was about 20ft. they left the tree and grass looking a mess, the boss gives my sister a Holly wreath.

A customer came into the shop and asked me, which bin do you put the cellophane in?? I said "there is no way of recycling cellophane you will have to bin it. She started having a go at me saying it's all your fault they are making all this cellophane I smiled and walked away.

Later that week there was another lady what said to me can I have 2 red Roses I thought, I would put them in some cellophane. The customer started to say she is going to throw them in the sea, she started to say we don't need any more cellophane in the sea like it was my fault.

A colleague and I were at a wedding venue, they had a basement we were taking some things down the stairs, but I was always ended up going down the stairs backwards. If I lost my footing I would have been at the bottom of the stairs not telling this story.

<u>Asymmetrical Arrangements</u>

An asymmetrical arrangement means an L shaped arrangement.

<u>You will need</u>

Floral foam /A container // Pot tape

Foliages e.g. Palm leaves, Salal and Eucalyptus

Flowers- Roses, Carnations, Lilies, Lisanthus and Carnation Spray

<u>Construction</u>

Soak you floral foam tape it onto your container and use the Palm leaf the back of the design to create height. Then put another palm leaf at the bottom right so you are creating an L shape with the palms then fill in the rest of the floral foam in-between the palms not straying from that shape.

Then add in more tall foliage such as Eucalyptus until you have a good shape to place the flowers in. Add the budded Lilies to the top of the design go down the design adding the other flowers in a line, place some open Lilies for the centre of the design then put some lilies coming out where the other Palm is placed to create the L Shape. On the right side place, shorter flower stems to define the L shape, fill in with foliage to cover any floral foam showing.

<u>Symmetrical arrangement</u>

The only difference between asymmetrical and symmetrical this design is a triangle shape

When making this design make a triangle shape or symmetrical shape, you are aiming for the design to have the same flowers on either side of the design.

<u>Construction</u>

Give it some height with the Palms then with the other 2 palms put them on at the bottom other design at the left and the right making a triangle shape with the foliage then fill the rest of the design with the foliage.

Then you go along with the same idea with the asymmetrical design put the flowers in a line but then you follow the foliage you have a place in this design creating a triangle shape.

This design is often used in churches at the front for weddings for a grand arrangement.

One Christmas I was going to put some decorations up on a Christmas tree at the florist. I got the tall ladder because I needed to get to the top of the tree. I put the decorations on the tree, the ladder started to fall to the left so I grabbed the Christmas tree. I knew, I was going down I knocked into the flower stand and the plastic vases fell off with the flowers in them of course. I sorted it all out but because nobody was holding the ladder for me. I walked into the workroom and my boss said if I can't trust you to go up a ladder you will have to go.

I had to climb into an industrial bin at the florist to flatten down the rubbish on one occasion, I was getting out of the bin and I fell onto the floor "Ouch" two men were walking past, but didn't seem to notice!

On another occasion, I was flattening the cardboard down, and there was hardly anything in the bin. I lost my footing and ended up at the bottom of the bin "Embarrassing"

A colleague was right underneath, minding her own business when some mettle off the walkway above her head broke off and fell into the bin beside her. If she had moved an inch, she could have been killed because there was no-one around to tell her to move.

I was on a delivery one day, I knocked on the customer's door a voice came from the back of the house. Saying go to the side gate, I went to the gate with the flowers then three big dogs came running to the gate barking at me. I was so shocked by these dogs, I gave the flowers to the woman and went straight back to the van.

A customer came into the shop, I help him he started to stutter on his words, when I was taking his order I didn't presume what he was going to say. I had finished taking the order he thanked me for not taking over when he spoke. My colleagues said how good I was. This taught me to be more patient.

There was a man who always came into the florist shop, he asked me for one Carnation in a plastic test tube wrapped in cellophane. So I asked my Colleague why he did this, they told me that he is a lollypop man and on the way to work some years ago he had an accident and knocked a small child over unfortunately the child died. Ever since that day he has bought a Carnation to put on the child's grave.

One day I went to work, the boss said to everyone "there has been an occasion when everyone was talking instead of working". So I went to do some work without clocking in and I came back after 1hour I clocked in. Later I was told I was going to take a wedding order with the boss and she told me in the van "you were the only one who was working".

There was one occasion when I came into the florist, I was just about to start work when I discovered that there was no water coming out of the tap. As you will know florists can't work without any water. Thankfully the water returned after 2 hours. On another occasion, there was a power cut so, we had no lights or phones. Not a good situation as you can't run a business without these things

A man came into the shop and asked me if he could have a hand-tied so I showed him the handtieds in boxes and gift wraps not in water. The customer said he didn't like them so he asked could he pick some flowers,

I replied yes so he started grouping the flowers?? I was thinking what is he doing. He perks up and says do you like what I have done so I replied yes there are so many different types of floristry, I was thinking it looked awful. I told my manageress what he was doing she said it must be in there culture to do that. I wrapped it up in the brown paper the customer says about the Roses not smelling so I said not a lot of roses that do smell and the ones that smell we don't have at the moment. I think he was Indian, he was very nervous he spilt his coffee all over the floor he said to me he was going to declare his love to a woman. When he asked my Manageress what do think of my flowers she said they were nice when he was gone, she said I wouldn't put my name to them. He came back the following week and told us about how it went the person who he went to declare his love too didn't feel the same!!

There was a funeral order that said on it "Toy plane to be added", the customer hadn't brought anything in for it. We were foxed because it was about 4.00 pm on Saturday. There were 3 of us in, the driver had gone for the day, so my colleague rang her son because he had some model planes so he brought his least favourite plane in.

Chapter four
Wedding Design's
&
Wedding stories
<u>Wedding Designs</u>

With Wedding floristry, it changes all the time i.e. like in 2010 they liked mettle work making different shapes and aluminium wire the flowers are glue on.

I didn't like it myself but it was conserved modern for that time
When you are taking a wedding order you have to take into the perspective of the couple you are talking to.

They will bring you different magazines and different ideas, they will expect you to transform into their dream day.

The easiest way to do this is to show them some of your pictures and work out a price

If they are looking at flowers that are out of season or flowers that are hard to get a hold of, let them know.

There are different styles such as modern or traditional, with modern weddings you can show them tropical designs with traditional weddings people like candelabras with old fashioned flowers such as Roses that smell and scented flowers. Country garden wedding's most people want flowers that look like they have been just picked from there garden or a wildflower meadow.

When you are doing for this sort of design make it look as natural as possible

with this style there are jam jars, birdcage you don't have to make everyone look the same or you lose the overall appeal.

When you have got the style and the colour it comes down to the price, write the price and the quantity for each design the customers wants.

Go through it all with them how big they want the designs and how much they want to spend and if you can make it to their budget.

<u>Wedding</u>

<u>Bridal work - Buttonholes</u>

<u>You will need</u>

1- Rose, foliage e.g. Hard Ruckus, 3 silver wires thin, 1 1- Green wire, and Parafilm or paper tape

<u>Construction</u>

There is quite a lot of different flowers you can make into a buttonhole main flowers such as Roses, Carnations these are main flowers people use for them.

You will need to cut the Rose head off and allow 2 fingers worth of stem, use the thick green wire cut it so you have 3 fingers worth of wire in the stem and outside the stem.

When you are putting it up the stem don't put it up to fast or too much because you will break the stem or bruise the Rose. Cut the wire so the wire isn't sharp lastly you need to get the Parafilm to keep it warm because when you stretch it. Wire some foliage e.g. Hard Ruckus brake 3 leaves off, wire them by putting the wire through the middle of the leaf fold the wire back on its self bring it back down to the stem and tape it. Do this 3 times and construct your button hole by putting the leaves around your Rose then wrap your Parofilm around the stem until it becomes thinner so you start at the top of the stem, wrap it around it and pull and twist the flower so you are going down the stem until you get down to the bottom of the wire you are putting this on because it will hold in moister.

Then spray it with water or flower food spray you need to keep the buttonhole in a cool place

into a garage or the hall out of direct sunlight but not in a fridge.

<u>Corsages</u>

The only difference between buttonholes and corsages you use more delicate flowers and you put more flowers into them, you can attach them onto a wrist corsage such as a ribbon.

<u>Wedding</u>

When you think of a wedding you think of amazing flowers and wonderful venues well florists do but at the beginning, you have to think plan and preparation and good relationship with people at the venues.

Planning usually consists of when the flowers are going to come, how many flower to put in each design. When to deliver the brides flowers to the house then the arrangements to the venues to set the tables and make the venue look absolutely amazing with the design that the florist has made.

When you are going to a wedding venue be prepared for anything to go wrong so you take your toolbox when you are at the venues. With the flowers, you need to prepare the flowers so they are going to be at the right stage for the wedding such as Roses you want them open but you don't want them open too much it is knowing when to make the design when the flowers are perfect to use. The last stage is easy making the flower arrangements well I think this is the best part of preparing a wedding.

<u>Wedding</u>
<u>Traditional wedding</u>
<u>Candelabra Arrangement</u>
<u>You will need</u>
Candelabra 4 tapered candles , 2 wreath rings backed with foam
String , Orchid sticks , Soft foliage such as Eucalyptus, Soft Ruckus
Delicate flowers such as Roses, Lisanthus, Stocks, Spray Roses,
Singapore Orchids

<u>Construction</u>

To start you first soak the wreath rings attach it to the candelabra by putting it through the central candle holder with the floral foam at the top and tie it onto the candelabra with string. Next, do the same by putting another wreath ring underneath the candelabra arms and tie it onto the candelabra then put the orchid stick to keep the wreaths in place.

Next is creating the arrangement

Add the foliage into the bottom wreath ring keeping the foliage tight to the candelabra with soft foliages such as Asparagus Densiflorus adding Eucalyptus Baby Blue which gives a delicate and streamlined shape. Work your way up to the top of the design to make a ball shape keeping all the flowing foliages low as you have to think you are going to put candles on this design.

<u>Candelabra Arrangement</u>

<u>Construction part 2</u>

Flowers

Start with the flowers going down the candelabra use budded flowers such as Lisanthus, when you are working up to use the Stocks "Mattiola Incana" keeping the flowers with good space and line in-between each flower then when you get to the main part of the design the ball shape place the Roses keeping them nicely spaced out adding Lisanthus and the Spray Roses though the middle of them.

There was another occasion at a venue I gave a box of 20 buttonholes to the barman at this venue he said to me I will put them somewhere safe and I found out when the wedding was over the bride and groom were giving their feedback about the venue and said they had lost the box of buttonholes.

Once, I was making some buttonholes for a wedding. I wasn't the one who dealt with the customer when ordering them. If I had been, I would have tried to persuade her not to have what she'd asked for, which was six orange Germini buttonholes. However, I made them up, and the customer said to me, "The Germini is the wrong colour". She wanted the colour at the back of the flower, so I had to tell her that there wasn't any Germini of that colour.

Sometimes I had to drop things off at wedding receptions, which often involved climbing stairs. Often the easiest way to load up a lift with all the things, to stop the lift doors from closing I had to use a fire extinguisher. Then I had to squeeze in with all the stands, flowers etc. It was a tight squeeze. At the top, I had to take everything out. Leave the things near the lift doors, then repeat this process until everything was upstairs. Collecting the items again, to take back to the shop, including the unwanted flowers, involved doing the something again in reverse, and then get it all back into the van to take back to the shop.

<u>Wedding</u>

<u>A vase arrangement</u>

There are lots of different types of vases you can use in wedding arrangements and different ways you can use them

You can put designs on top of the vase then you can make something and place it inside the vase.

Martini vases there are all sorts of different sizes I have done them for a table centre

If there are a lot of different containers and vases to choose from

But you have to think, with containers tall thin so the flowers are above the heads of the guests or small containers close to the table so the guests can see over the arrangement's to see each other.

On one occasion, I wouldn't want to repeat, I went to deliver some wedding 2 stand arrangements at the local church. I put the flowers stands where I had been told the bride wanted them in the church. A lady appeared, who was a church steward, and told me, "You can't move the church flowers. You will have to put the wedding flowers somewhere else" This lady certainly had an attitude, so I left the boss to deal with it. If anyone could sort her out, it would be my boss, so I went back to the shop to get her.

I was at a wedding venue, with two other colleagues and I was in charge, so I had to explain how to put a candle into a candelabra without breaking the candelabra. You put your hand under the arm of the candelabra you are putting the candle in. After explaining all of this one person said what do I do, I show her then I turned my back and discovered that she had put the candle into the candelabra without putting her hand under the arm. The result was a broken candelabra and everyone went back to the shop. I had to stay at the venue until they returned bringing another candelabra for me to put into the venue.

<u>Wedding -Top table Arrangement</u>

<u>You will need</u>

2 blocks of floral foam, Pot tape , a medium tray hold 2 floral foam ,soft following foliages such as Soft Ruckus, Palm leaves, Bear Grass, Roses, Lisanthus, Freesia, Veronica, Singapore Orchids

<u>Construction</u>

To start this design with the length depending on how big you want this design the usual size is 4ft, add Palms and soft Ruckus then have the front of the design coming over the table trailing about 1ft with the palms and soft Ruckus. The back of the design needs to be flat either fill this in with the foliages use the flowers from the design but not as many. You are going for a design like a double-ended but it is ½ of the design so it trails over the top table and it doesn't take over the table.

Adding the flowers you need to start with the length add the Singapore Orchids and the trailing part of the design then add the Roses and place them through the design evenly for the length and add them to trail down the design keeping space between the flowers then fill in with the Lisanthus and the Veronica. So you are left with a nice trailing design when you have finished the top table desgn fill in with any other foliages to make it trailing such as Bear Grass.

This design is the focal design so you need to match this to the table centres within the other designs

On my first wedding venue at this particular florist, I went with my colleague to this Hall. I first got the goldfish bowls out and cleaned them because they hadn't been cleaned?? Then I got a watering can and filled every goldfish bowl, we had to put funny rubber ducks into the bowls. There were all kinds of ducks Star wars- Darth ducks, anything you can imagine. The thing was they wouldn't stay upright, so we had to take them out, dry them and put them back in when we had done this the all stayed upright and looked amazing.

A new person who had started at the florist he was there for a few months. He was putting white candelabras into a bucket they were made up with red Roses. I would usually put them into a Dutch bucket which is smaller than the one he was using. The bucket he was using had ridges at the bottom. So I told him to "put them in the other buckets" so he replied by saying " I know what I am doing". So I left him to it. So later I was told I was going with my other colleague to the wedding venue. We were going to use the old Jeep, to take the Candelabra arrangements. The old Jeep was jerking about. "This was bad enough" we arrived at the venue and all the Candelabra's had fallen over " because they weren't secure just as I thought". So my colleague said "Don't panic Just get them out and sort them out because the flowers had fallen out the arrangements" so we dealt with it and carried on as normal.

<u>Wedding</u>
<u>Garland</u>

There are 2 different ways of doing a garland

One way is using a floral foam snake which you soak it onsite were the wedding is and attach it to the entrance of the building that the wedding party is going to go into either the church door or venue door.

Make the design onsite so you have more freedom to make the design with it attached to the wall so the Garland can flow with soft foliages and have flowers that are small like any sort of Orchids, Large Roses so people can see the flowers Lisanthus and foliage going though the Garland. When you have finished the design, spray it to keep it fresh.

The second way is just to use Soft Ruckus, Trailing Ivy and other foliage and bind them together with binding wire to create a long snake shape then you can add it to where you are going to put the garland. I have used them going on banisters as they don't have anything to drip and they are dry the venue will allow them in the building.

<u>Wedding</u>
<u>Bridal work-Shower Bouquets</u>
There are 2 ways of doing these all wired
In foam, you wire some of it and glue the rest in
<u>Wired</u>
I will tell you how to do a wired one usually get flowers that fall nicely very light flowers such as Calla lilies Roses for the focal flowers then add in other flowers such as Lisanthus and mix it with other flowers. So with all these flowers, you will need to wire them individually then the shape you will be aiming for is a teardrop shape.
The wired bouquets are for a more experienced florist.
In floral foam
The difference is you have to wire the length and pull the wire and bend it back on its self so it is secure then you glue everything else into making a teardrop shape.
<u>Wedding</u>
<u>Bridal work</u>
<u>Wand</u>
Wands are usually given to bridesmaids that are children
<u>You will need</u>
Coloured Aluminium wire, Flowers e.g. Roses, Cymbidium Orchids, Wire to wire the flower, Parafilm, coloured bullion wire. Beads
<u>Construction</u>
Wire and tape the Orchid e.g. Cymbidium place your thin green wire up the stem until you are at the top of the flower but don't go up to high because you will break the Orchid head next where you have wired the flowers use the Parafilm place it at the top of the stem and keep it on the stem then pull the tape down gradually so you don't snap it so you are pulling the tape and twisting the flower until you have sealed the stem.
Keep the length of the wire stem, next make a nest out of coloured aluminium wire so you have both the aluminium wire and the flower you wired to feed the wire through the nest so it is resting in the middle

securely. When you have done this tape both the wires together with the Parafilm as above until you have taped it to the end of the wire. To finish the wand us the coloured bullion wire so it matches the coloured aluminium wire wrap it around your stem if you want to add beads down the stem. You could add beads onto your bullion wire for added interest.

Wedding
Bridal work
Handtied for a wedding

Brides and Bridesmaids- usually have handtieds, the bridesmaid's designs are not as elaborate as the brides. Bride's flowers need to be more impressive than the bridesmaids.

Usually when you are planning how to make the bridesmaids handtieds, keep the flowers all one flowers such as Roses. The Brides flowers have the same Roses but add a mixture of more delicate flowers. When making Bridal handtieds there are more things you have to bear in mind such as if you are using Roses. The Roses need to be at their best, by this I mean you need to buy them about a week in advance and cut them and put them in some water then a few days before you are going to make them cut them down to the length you are going to use for the hand-tied. Keep an eye on them to make sure they don't open too much.

You then have a good size Rose that looks better than a tight bud Keep all the stems clear and tidy taking any thorns or leaves off that don't need to be on.

When making Bridal Handtieds such as a mixed flower design keep them more compact add foliage in-between such as Eucalyptus or hard Ruckus each time you add a flower then finish off by putting foliage around the edge of the bouquet. If you are doing an all Rose Bridal Handtied keep all the flowers compact and tight together There are two ways of doing this Add foliage in-between the flowers to make it look bigger.

Sometimes florists don't put foliage in-between the Roses it all depends what style you are going for. You can also add pearl headed pins or diamond headed pins in the centre of the Rose heads you could also add beads on a wire to go in-between the Roses.

<u>Making a hand-tied for a Wedding</u>

<u>You will need</u>

Mixture of flowers e.g. Roses, Orchids, Lisanthus, Astrantia major. Eucalyptus or hard Ruckus. If you are making an all one flower design all one flower Orchids such as Cymbidium, Rose's, Gerbera's

<u>Construction</u>

Start the Handtied with your central flower then add some foliage then put you next flower next to the first one but at an angle turn the design 360 degrease so you are turning the stems so they aren't crossing. But with wedding handtieds, you need to keep the heads of the flowers more compact so they are more together adding the foliage each time you add a flower.

It is the same if you are making an all one flower design keep adding the flowers and use the same technique with turning the design around.

<u>To finish off a wedding hand-tied</u>

Make sure your design is tied tight but not too tight have the flowers so the flowers aren't squashed.

When you have tied it off use some plastic ribbon going with the colour of flowers you have chosen. Bind it about ½ the stems keeping it tight and consistent. When you get to the point where you are going to finish wrapping it around the stems see if the ribbon has a straight line all the way around, when you have done this fold the ribbon so it is double for the end then tape it with cello tape then have some satin or organiser ribbon that matches the other ribbon so you can't see through it, take the wire out of the ribbon of the organiser or satin ribbon and bind it the same way around the first ribbon until you get to the end and fold it over. Place pearl headed pins in there is a knack to this you need to place the pins in so they are pushed up so they are going through the stems. So no one can feel the sharp end of the pin so firstly put the first pin at the top of the ribbon then the second ribbon in the middle and then one last one at the bottom keeping them in a line then fill 2 pins in-between each pin.

<u>Floral Foam Bag</u>

<u>You will need</u>

Floral foam, Lamb's Ears "Stachys Byzantina leaves" or Elaeagnus Pungnus "Maculata", pearl headed pins, beads, long thick wire and coloured string, bobbin wire coloured, flowers

<u>Construction</u>

Make your floral foam small bag shape roughly 1/2 a block of floral foam soak the top to give it some weight, next cover 2 thick wire by wrapping the coloured string around the wire and attaching it with some beads on some coloured bullion wire to keep the string in place. Keep enough at the ends of the wire so you can put them through the floral foam and secure into the floral foam so the wires become your handles of the bag.

The next part of the design is attaching the leaves onto the bag design, hold the leaves facing downwards then pin them in place keep the leaves tight together overlap them.

Do this until you have finished the design cover the bottom of the bag doing the same principle

To create some interest

Attach some flowers at the top of the design underneath the handle making a nice design.

Chapter 5 Materials used in the floristry industry &About floral foam

<u>Some products we use in the floristry industry</u>

Wires for wiring flowers

70g – for wiring flowers – for buttonholes

Thin wire- for foliage for buttonholes

100g Parafilm – paper tape.

Bobbin wire for Christmas

Floral foam's when using floral foam were gloves when picking it up and a mask when cutting it.

Posy pad veering sizes you can get every different shape you want even letters.

Wired wreath ring – you can get different sizes 10inch, 12inch, 14inch.

Wires 24g

Bullion wire coloured 0.3mm x 25g you can get different colours

Aluminium wire coloured

Pot tape you can get thick and thin

German Pins

Perl headed pins "I usually use the 4mm head and 4cm long"

Floristry scissors "the difference between normal scissors and florist scissors are sharper"

Craft paper for wrapping your flowers into

Used

ECO Bio Base Compostable Cellophane

Pin holders

When making a small arrangement

Use the oasis fix to stick it

Chicken wire is used natural arrangements use 1ft and squash it together to fit inside your vase or container may need to secure with pot tape

<u>Floral Foam</u>

I have been doing some research and there are a lot of chemicals that go into the floral foam

<u>Such as</u>

1.   Phenol-formaldehyde which can break down into Microplastics are eaten by a marine and freshwater invertebrate. Other than that it isn't good to touch floral foam because it has this toxic chemical in it which it can cause cancer to your skin if you constantly touch it, breathing in the dust partials isn't healthy either.

1.   When the floral foam brakes down it cause oxides, carbon and it causes such as carbon monoxide CO and carbon dioxide CO2.

1.   "Carbon black

Is a carcinogenic to humans in the short-term exposure in high concentrations it can cause cancer?

When you have soaked the floral foam pouring the liquid down the drain all these chemicals will go into the water supply not just effecting marine life but could affect us down the line as well.

<u>Floral foam</u>

<u>I have attached some website to this page from my research</u>

Chelsea Flower show is banning Floral foam

https://www.countryliving.com/uk/homes-interiors/gardens/a30622511/chelsea-flower-show-rhs-ban-floralfoam/#:~:text=Floral%20foam%20is%20a%20synthetic,always%20essent

<u>https://www.cancer.org/cancer/cancer-causes/formaldehyde.html</u>

https://en.wikipedia.org/wiki/Carbon_black
There is a book about the effect of this on marine life called Science of the total environment

Below is a book about the effect on the environment
https://www.sciencedirect.com/science/article/pii/S0048969719358218?via%3Dihub

I have looked into other florists around the world and some countries have stopped people from using floral foam because of the effects on the environment
Floral Foam
There is a website you can go to
https://www.instagram.com/nofloralfoam/?hl=en
https://sustainablefloristry.org/
If you look at Australia and Europe they know what the effects are when using floral foam on the environment. Quite allot have stopped using floral foam and are going back to the methods that were used before floral foam was made.
Making the base for the funeral design using sticks, mettle and binding the moss onto it to create the desired shape. When wiring the flowers into Moss to keep them secure.
Look into different designs, you can make designs using renewable sources e.g. using moss in a bamboo container with chicken wire over the moss and wiring it to keep it securely fixed to the container.
But most florists in the UK don't know about floral foam being bad for the environment or bad for their health or they wouldn't use it. I have used floral foam for 16 years, I don't know what the long term damage is.

I have gone into the biodegradable floral foam as well and that still brakes down into CO2 and methane which is still not good for the environment.

The best thing is to go back to a sustainable sourced Moss.

A lady came into the shop on a Sunday, When I was in charge, the lady
     Said to me can I have a traditional handtied at £25.00. A handtied in
water with
     All Carnation spray, My heart sank at this point I went around
the shop and went thought all the flowers such as Carnations ,
Chrysanthemum blooms there wasn't a lot of flowers as the flowers come
on Monday.

Then another customer came in and asked could I have a contempary
handtied no Carnations, Chrysanthemums EST. Just Modern flowers
I hadn't even written out the previous order, well I went through the
flowers. I went back into the workroom I wrote the 2 orders out. I had
to write down all the flowers the lady wanted but she only wanted to
spend £25 in flower terms that is not a lot in the florist. So I did the
first handtied's. So I did the first handtied's when I had finished it was
Horrible I hadn't done a handtied's with just Carnations , Carnation
spray & Chrysanthemums "Well I didn't like it but she did" Then I made
the modern handtied's and I loved it "

Two orders completely different you have to think on your feet. If
the customer is unpleasant just smile and carry on don't let upset you
or effect you serve them. The same week there was another unpleasant
customer said to me when I was showing another customer around the
shop, he said in very abrupt manner. "My mum doesn't like most of the
flowers you have got in the shop. I finished serving the first customer.
Then I had to write a list of all of the flowers all that I couldn't use for
the second customer, Lilies, Carnations ,est. then he ended the order
by saying to me "You get the message" Wow people can be so rude.
Thankfully when I had made the handtieds he loved it. "But the question
is did his mum".

The same day I had to follow up an order that the boss had left for
me. She couldn't get the order though the Interflora system so I had to
phone the Customer. She was horrible with me I was just trying to get
the address out of her. It was an Interflora order the lady said to me

"just cancel the order, because I don't know the full address, this order has been a pain", then she said to me "I am driving"!! , So I said to her "Should I try putting the order though the Interflora system again" she said. "No" So I left the order and a few hours later my boss came in and tried again to phone her and she wasn't very nice with him even when he tried to fix the situation by offering her something she was still not very nice so we had to void the order.

(Check out Floristry book 2 lots of photos of how to make the things and on my website I have got a online floristry course come and have a look)

<u>Check out all our other books</u> <u>https://heartloveart.wixsite.com/</u><u>website/philip-stanworth-author-all-books</u>[1]

The website is on this QR code

All my socials, all about Philip Stanworth and all my eBook and print book and all the stores you can buy them are all linked to my website above.

There are even Toys, children's clothes, bags and more on my website check it out.

---

1.   https://heartloveart.wixsite.com/%20website/philip-stanworth-author-all-books

<u>**Books Written by**</u>
<u>**Philip Stanworth books &**</u>
<u>**N Stanworth's books**</u>
You Think You Want To Be A Florist Part One
You Think You Want To Be A Florist Part Two
<u>**Children's books**</u>
Alphabet & Numbers
A Small Snapshot of Birds
The Good Shepherd & Other Stories
The Mansion Through Time Part one
Surprise Days Out With The Kids

All the books

Also by Philip Stanworth

All The books together
A Small Snapshot Of Birds
You Think You Want To Be A Florist Part one
You Think You Want To Be A Florist Part 2
The Good Shepherd & Other Stories
Surprise Days Out With The Kids
The Mansion Through Time
Three Small Stories for 3-4 year olds
Alphabet & Numbers

Standalone
You Think You Want To Be A Florist

Watch for more at https://designs-by-nature.teemill.com/.